The Burden Of Isis

by

James Teackle Dennis

Double 9 BOOKS

The Burden Of Isis
by James Teackle Dennis

ISBN: 978-93-59393-87-2

Published by

DOUBLE 9 BOOKS
2/13-B, Ansari Road
Daryaganj, New Delhi – 110002
info@double9books.com
www.double9books.com
Tel. 011-40042856

ABOUT THE AUTHOR

James Teackle Dennis is an esteemed author renowned for his compelling works in the realm of historical fiction and mythology. Born with a passion for storytelling, Dennis has dedicated his career to bringing the past to life through rich narratives and meticulous research. While information about James Teackle Dennis's personal life remains scarce, his literary contributions have left an indelible mark on the literary world. With a keen interest in ancient civilizations, particularly Egypt, Dennis has delved deep into the annals of history to unearth forgotten tales and unravel the mysteries of the past. James Teackle Dennis's contributions to the literary world have garnered him a loyal following of readers who appreciate his ability to transport them to different times and places. While the personal details of James Teackle Dennis's life may remain shrouded in mystery, his literary legacy as a masterful storyteller and historian endures.

CONTENTS

Introduction

OF all the Egyptian religious beliefs that existed from the Prehistoric period down into Roman times, the oldest and the one most held in veneration was that connected with the worship of Osiris, Isis and Horus. These three, though primarily only local gods, at an. early period became prominent deities of all Egypt; and the cult of Isis, more particularly, remained a favourite always, rivalling even that of Osiris in later times.

During the many thousand years of Egyptian history, not only did many changes occur in the ceremonies connected with these cults, but also the legends and origin of the Osirian faith received many additions and interpolations; and thus the old faith lost much of its purity. The simplest form in which it is preserved to us states that Osiris was the son of Seb and Nut--*i.e.* Earth and Heaven; of whom were born also Isis, Nephthys and Set, or Sutekh, as he is also called,

Osiris married his sister Isis, while Set chose Nephthys. It is probably due to this feature of the legend that the Pharaohs often married their sisters, and occasionally also their daughters. Osiris was the first divine ruler of Egypt: whence he came is not told; but when he came to that country, he found it sunk in barbarism and ignorance, with no law but that of strength, and poverty everywhere. He went through the land settling quarrels, organizing government, teaching polite manners and customs, dictating laws and civilizing the people.

Set, his brother, became jealous of the renown of Osiris, and hated him because of the good he had done; and resolved upon his destruction. Assisted by the evil spirits, or demons (the "enemies" or "foes" of the chants), Set constructed a large chest exactly the size and shape of the body of his brother Osiris; and at a feast given by the latter, he offered to present the chest, which was richly adorned, to the one whose body it best fitted. No one was successful until Osiris entered the chest, when Set closed it, and with the help of the evil spirits bore it from the banquet hall and cast it into the Nile. Thereupon Isis fled to the Delta, taking with her Horus, her son, whom she left to be cared for in Buto, according to some legends; others say he was left with Tehuti, or Thoth, god of learning. Isis then took a boat and searched the Nile for the body of her husband, which she ultimately found in the Delta. Before it could be interred, however, it was stolen by Set, who then divided the body into fourteen portions, and scattered them over the whole of Egypt. Again the bereaved Isis commenced a search for the pieces of her husband's body, and found thirteen; the fourteenth piece, the phallus, she was unable to find, it having been eaten by fish.

Wherever a fragment of the body of Osiris was found, a temple was there erected to his memory; and as the head (or according to some authorities, the heart) was found at Abydos, that city was considered as especially sacred, and was the centre of his worship.

Horus, son of Osiris and Isis, avenged his father's death by ultimately slaying Set; while Osiris, miraculously resurrected by Horus in the regions of the dead, ruled over the underworld and its inhabitants. Such, briefly, is the legend of Osiris. But the cult could never have become national in character without changing in many ways. Every city and town of any prominence in Egypt had its own especial local deity, who received special worship, even while other deities were admitted to exist, though considered subordinate to him: and at an early date the priesthood of Osiris began systematically to identify the leading characteristics of these various local gods with those of Osiris. Hence in course of time we find Osiris-Sokar, an identification of the local god Sokar with the great deity of Abydos; Osiris-Apis, which in Greek times became Serapis, where the attributes of Osiris had become identified with those of a Memphite deity; and in later times, Osiris became a solar deity, and is addressed by epithets and titles which seem to show an identification with Ra, the sun god. By this means, Abydos became the great early religious centre of Egypt. But these identifications of various deities were not confined to Osiris. Horus became mutated, and gained new attributes--as Horus-Ra, he became the midday sun; and under the priesthood of Heliopolis, he became Tum, the setting sun, even losing his name. Isis, also, received new qualifications, being often identified with Hathor (whom the Greeks in turn identified with Aphrodite); but the chief places where Hathor was worshipped were at Dendereh and at Der-el-Bahri, in the western portion of Thebes; while the worship of Isis centred around Abydos and Busiris, the latter being frequently mentioned in the liturgies; and in later times also she was worshipped at Philae; and her worship was so popular, that long after Egypt had ceased to be a nation, and her gods had become a by-word, there were no less than three great temples erected to her cult within the walls of Rome itself.

It is this merging of the attributes of one god into those of another, and their unification into Osiris, to which the chants refer when speaking of the "attributes" of the deities. The eating of the fourteenth fragment of the body of Osiris by fish is paralleled by a similar legend in the story of "Anpu and Bata," often called the "Tale of the Two Brothers."

The triad was not an unusual combination in the Egyptian belief; for besides that of Osiris, Isis and Horus, we find Amen, Mut and Khonsu at Thebes; and other lesser triads; so that when Christianity reached Egypt, the trinitarian idea found ready adherents; and this may partly account for the strides which Christianity made in Egypt almost before it had obtained a foothold elsewhere. The resurrection of Osiris and his ruling over the spirits of the deceased is nearly a parallel to the story of the Cretan King Minos, and possesses some points in common with the Christian belief; while the worship of Isis paved the way for the worship of the Virgin Mary many centuries later, though this latter was repudiated by the Egyptian Christians of the first four centuries, probably as being too reminiscent of "paganism." (Budge, "Paradise of the Fathers," I., II.)

The position of Set is curious. While he was considered an evil deity, yet he had many temples and worshippers; in early times, strangely enough, in addition to the "Horus" name, some Pharaohs had a "Set" name; and the name of Set was used by several later Pharaohs, such as Sety I., Sety Merenptah, Set-aa-pehti, Set-Nekht and others.

Nephthys plays a somewhat unimportant rôle in the liturgies, as well as in the Egyptian pantheon, being usually associated with Isis. She seems to have repudiated Set after the murder of Osiris, and to have aided Isis in seeking for the body.

The continuity of the chants is much broken it appears as if two, or even three, deities are addressed at the same moment. This, however is due to two causes: first, the identification of attributes originally belonging to divers deities in the person of the one god Osiris; and second, to the fact that these chants were accompanied by spectacular performances--a forerunner of the "miracle-plays" of the Elizabethan period. Various temple officials impersonated the gods on certain occasions, and these were implored, invoked or praised as the living representative of the deity. But more frequently the animal sacred to the god was brought out and worshipped--not for himself, but for the deity he represented. The Hawk of Horus at Edfu, the Crocodile of Sebek at Crocodilopolis, the Cow of Hathor, the

Bull Apis--all were praised as the living counterpart chosen by the god to represent himself. And just as in Roman Catholic churches, at certain times, a bell was formerly rung to frighten away the Devil, so in the Egyptian time the sistrum-bearer was prominent at sacred festivals; for it was his duty, by shaking the sistrum, not to frighten the evil one, but to call the attention of the deity specially to his worshippers. This accounts for the frequent appeal in the liturgies--"Behold the excellent sistrum-bearer!"

What will most impress one in these liturgies, however, is the deep, sincere religious feeling that permeates them--the grief for the lost one, the hope of again beholding him, the cry from the heart for help, the reliance upon the divine all-ruling destiny that shall bring the trial to a happy ending, and the triumph of a desire realized and a hope fulfilled: these sentiments, as much a part of human nature now as then, bring the far-off dwellers of the land of Kem near at heart and feeling to the twentieth-century reader of our own era. For above all nations of old, the future life entered especially into the Egyptian daily life and thought; their religion was one where the present was considered only the threshold; and it was their belief in the absolute endlessness of matter and the immortality of the spirit that causes the frequent formula after many of their names--"Ankh zetta heh"--living for ever, eternal.

The two papyri in which these chants are found were both discovered in Luxor, Egypt; and that relating particularly to Osiris is written in a hand representing an intermediate stage between hieratic and demotic. The chants of Isis were found inside a statue of Osiris, by M. Passalaqua.

The period when these chants were first written is unknown. Probably in the earliest times, they were committed to memory, and handed down verbally from generation to generation, as were so many traditions of olden time.

We may believe, however, that they had already been reduced to writing by the time of the fourth dynasty, though at that time they probably consisted chiefly of the invocatory portions, the subsidiary matter being added later, and at different periods.

The date of the texts from which the present translations are made approximates 300 B.C., while the texts themselves are written in a purer and more classic style than are most of the writings of that time; so that it is probable that in their present form they certainly are; not later than the twenty-sixth dynasty, and may probably be as early as the eighteenth or nineteenth.

The Osiris chant, together with one of the Isis and Nephthys liturgies, exists in the hieratic form in what is known as the "Rhind papyrus," B.M. 10188, while the other Isis liturgy is in the Berlin papyrus 14225. Extracts have been published by Pleyte, in "Recueil des Travaux," Vol. III., and by Dr. E. A. Wallis Budge in Vol. LII. of "Archaeologia," many years ago. De Horrack published the second Isis liturgy in French, a translation of which into English appeared in "Records of the Past," Vol. II. The three chants, however, have not heretofore been published in one volume.

From the frequent mention of the sistrum-bearer in the chants, we know that this musical instrument was chiefly employed, but the music in which they were written is unknown. The Egyptians rated music highly, and Plato considered their music superior to the Greek, both for melody and energy. But harmony and rhythm were always subordinated to the words, and the subject-matter was paramount. There were two sorts of harmonies known to the old Egyptians, which the Greeks designated as "Dorian" and "Phrygian"--the former grave, slow and tranquil, the latter a dithyrambic form, probably employed in these chants, which was forceful, appealing and energetic.

The Egyptians based their music on seven diatonics, which Demetrius of Phalerus attributes to "the seven vowels"; others say the seven senses, or the seven planets. Dion Cassius corroborates him, while Dionysos of Halicarnassus says, "Melody embraced an interval of five-it never rose more than three and one-half tones toward high, and fell less toward bass." This probably was a result of the use of the three-stringed lyre.

To find a probable origin for the legend of Osiris and Isis, it may seem strange to have to turn to the shores of Mexico and Central America; yet there, among the ruined cities of the ancient Mayan civilization, according to Le Plongeon, are two temples bearing historical inscriptions which in many details correspond with the Egyptian legend. The king, ruling well and wisely, is slain and dismembered by his brother, and the sister-wife, after finding the body, erected over it a pyramid and sphinx, the latter with a human head on a leopard's body, after which she travelled eastward, to the colonies of her race that had settled there centuries before; where she lived until her death. Her son ultimately killed his usurping uncle, and ruled the Mayans in his stead. The points of resemblance between the two legends are too numerous to name here; but as the period when the Mayan events took place is about ten thousand years before Christ, if the legends arose from one common source it would give ample time for history to become merged into myth.

Whatever be the origin of the Osiris belief, however, it is certain that in the beginning he did not typify any of the forces of nature, as some would have us believe: this is a theory of much later date than the belief upon which it is grafted, and belongs to a period of decline; and Osiris is rather to be regarded as one of the great rulers of old time, far-seeing, advanced in his ideas, who fell a martyr to his duty, his conscience and his people. Had the Pharaohs tried rather to emulate the living Osiris, instead of simply being merged into him after death, Egypt might have survived for many centuries the cataclysms which eventually overwhelmed her, and put an end to her existence as a nation.

The Laments Of Isis And Nephthys

(BERLIN PAP. 1425)

INVOCATION concerning the glorious things done by the two goddesses of the temple of Osiris, Khent-Amentit,1 the great God of Abydos; performed in the 4th summer month, 25th day; likewise to be performed in every shrine of Osiris at every one of his Heb-festivals. 2

Glorify his soul! Establish his dead body!

Praise his spirit! Give breath to his nostrils and to his parched throat!

Give gladness unto the heart of Isis and to that of Nephthys;

Place Horus upon the throne of his Father

Give life, stability and power to Osiris Thentirti, 3

Born of the great forsaken one, she who is called also Pelses, the truthful--

Glorious are her acts, according to the words of the gods.

Behold now, Isis speaketh,--

Come to thy temple, come to thy temple, oh An! 4

Come to thy temple, for thine enemies are not

Behold the excellent sistrum-bearer--come to thy temple!

Lo I, thy sister, love thee--do not thou depart from me!

Behold Hunnu, 5 the beautiful one

Come to thy temple immediately--come to thy temple immediately! Behold thou my heart, which grieveth for thee;

Behold me seeking for thee--I am searching for thee to behold thee!

Lo, I am prevented from beholding thee--

I am prevented from beholding thee, oh An!

It is blessed to behold thee--come to the one who loveth thee!

Come to the one who loveth thee, oh thou who art beautiful, Un-Nofer,
6 deceased.

Come to thy sister--come to thy wife--

Come to thy wife, oh thou who makest the heart to rest.

I, thy sister, born of thy mother, go about to every temple of thine,

Yet thou comest not forth to me

Gods, and men before the face of the gods, are weeping for thee at the same time, when they behold me!

Lo, I invoke thee with wailing that reacheth high as heaven,--

Yet thou hearest not my voice. Lo I, thy sister, I love thee more than all the earth--

And thou lovest not another as thou dost thy sister--

Surely thou lovest not another as thou dost thy sister!

Behold now, Nephthys speaketh,--

Behold the excellent sistrum-bearer! Come to thy temple!

Cause thy heart to rejoice, for thy enemies are not!

All thy sister-goddesses are at thy side and behind thy couch,

Calling upon thee with weeping--yet thou art prostrate upon thy bed!

Hearken unto the beautiful words uttered by us and by every noble one among us!

Subdue thou every sorrow which is in the hearts of us thy sisters,

Oh thou strong one among the gods,--strong among men who behold thee!

We come before thee, oh prince, our lord

Live before us, desiring to behold thee

Turn not thou away thy face before us

Sweeten our hearts when we behold thee, oh prince!

Beautify our hearts when we behold thee

I, Nephthys, thy sister, I love thee:

Thy foes are subdued, there is not one remaining.

Lo, I am with thee; I shall protect thy limbs for ever, eternally.

Behold now, Isis speaketh,--

Praised be An 7 thou shinest upon us from heav'n every day,

Yet can we not behold thy beams.

Tehuti 8 protecteth thee, he causeth thy soul to be established within the Maadet boat, 9 by

the power of thy name of "Iah"!

Come to me; for I would behold thee and thy beauties by means of the Uazit eye,-- 10

By the power of thy name of "Lord of the six festivals"!

Thy royal attendants are by thy side, nor go they forth from thee;

Thou takest possession of heaven by the greatness of thy terrors, and by the power of thy name of "Prince of the fifteen festivals"!

Thou shinest upon us like Ra, the lord--

Glow thou above us like Tum.

Gods and men live when beholding thee-shine thou upon us;

Brighten thou the two lands; 11

The two horizons are fitted for thy pathways.

Gods together with men are with thee;

No harm cometh unto them from thy shining,

Nor from thy journeying in the celestial boat 12 above.

Thy enemies have ceased to be, for I am protecting thee, oh Ra, lord!

Come thou to us as a babe, thou first great Sun god.

Depart not from us who behold thee

There proceedeth from thee the strong Orion in heaven at evening, at the resting of every day!

Lo, it is I, at the approach of the Sothis period, who doth watch for him,

Nor will I leave off watching for him; for that which proceedeth from thee is revered.

An emanation from thee causeth life to gods and men, reptiles and animals, and they live by means thereof.

Come thou to us from thy chamber, in the day when thy soul begetteth emanations,--

The day when offerings upon offerings are made to thy spirit, which causeth the gods and men likewise to live.

Praise be to the Lord, for there is no god like unto thee, oh Tum! 13

Thy soul possesseth the earth, and thy likenesses the underworld;

Lo, it is prepared for and containeth thy hidden shrine.

Thy wife is ready to protect thee, and thy son Horus also, as prince of the lands.

Behold now, Nephthys speaketh,--

Behold the excellent sistrum-bearer! Come to thy temple, Un-Nofer, deceased,--come to Deddu! 14

Behold the bull, the begotten one!

Come thou to Anep (Mendes), the beloved enclosure!

Come to Khar! Come to the two Deddus (Mendes and Busiris), the place which thy soul loveth, and the souls of thy fathers likewise!

Thy son, thy child Horus, born of thy sister-goddesses, is before thy face.

It is I who doth illuminate and protect thee every day--

I will not depart from thee for ever

Oh, An, come thou to Sais, for thy name is "Sau" (protector)! 15

Come to Aper! Behold thou thy mother, Nut, oh thou lovely child!

Depart thou not from her! Come to her breasts; abundance is therein!

Thy sister, too, is beautiful, depart thou not from her, oh son!

Come to Sais, oh Osiris, and to Tarud,

She who is called also Nisep, born of Pelses, deceased!

Come to Aper, thy city, thy seat, and to the temple of Deb!

Thou shalt rest beside thy mother eternally

She preserveth thy limbs and procureth terror among thy enemies, for she protecteth thy members for ever.

Behold the excellent sistrum-bearer! Come to thy temple!

Come, behold thou thy son Horus as prince of gods and men;

He taketh possession of the cities and the nomes by the magnitude of his terrors;

Heaven and earth are filled with fear of him,

And the barbarians are submissive under his terrors. Thy children are among gods and men,

And the eastern and western horizons are among the attributes of thy producing;

Thy two sisters are at thy side, purifying thy soul,

And thy son Horus admitteth thine attributes. There cometh forth funereal and other offerings--beer, bulls and geese--for thee:

Tehuti proclaimeth thy Heb-festival, and invoketh thee with his protecting formulae;

Horus covereth thy limbs with his protections

Every day thy son Horus glorifieth thy spirit,

And he avengeth thy name by offerings for thy soul placed at thy secret shrine.

As for the gods, their arms bear libation vases for the purifying of thy spirit.

Come to thy children, oh prince, our lord, nor depart thou from them.

Lo! he comes!

1 A title of Osiris--"Within the underworld."

2 Heb--a special festival.

3 Thentirti--name of Osiris.

4 An, the sun (or moon) god.

5 Name of the sun god.

6 One of the titles of Osiris.

7 The sun god.

8 Thoth, God of Wisdom.

9 Sunset boat.

10 Magic eye of Osiris,--bringing health and happiness to wearer.

11 Upper and Lower Egypt.

12 Boat of Ra, sun god.

13 Tum or Atum--sun, father of Osiris, god of Heliopolis.

14 Mendes, not the celestial Deddu, is here meant.

15 A pun on the word "Sais."

The Chants

(B.M. PAP. 10188)

BEGINNING in front of the temples, during the Heb-festivals of Isis and Nephthys, and performed before the shrine of Osiris, Khent-Amentit, 16 the great God, lord of Abydos, in the 4th month of Inundation, on the 22nd day and continued to the 26th day. Purify all that which appertains to the temple; bring forth the utensils of the priestesses, who have performed the ablutions, their arms not being bared, their hair flowing over their shoulders and their heads crowned with woollen scarves; a musical instrument in their arms, and their names inscribed upon their shoulders, dedicated to the service of Isis and Nephthys. Let them utter praises in the temples according to this writing, before this God. Let them say,--

Behold the lord Osiris! (Repeat four times the formula.)

Is not his Kher-Heb priest 17 held in awe in this temple--great in heaven and great on earth? (Repeat four times the formula.)

Are not the two impersonators of the goddesses, and Hunnu, 18 the beautiful, approaching to thy shrine at this moment? (Repeat twice.)

Do we not behold the excellent sistrum-bearer approaching to thy temple and drawing nigh, though thou hast departed from us?

Lo, Hunnu, the beautiful, passeth over the land hourly and yearly, at his proper-season;

He, the purified image of his father Tenen, 19 the essence of deep mysteries:

He proceedeth from Tum, the most excellent lord:

Perfect is he, like his father, the eldest god born of the body of his mother!

Come thou to us with thy attributes

Let those among us who travel not thy path be embraced by thee:

Beautiful of face and greatly beloved is the image of Tenen, male lord of love, adored when he exhibiteth himself.

His limbs fail from his being bound;--

Come thou in peace, oh thou lord of those among us who behold the two goddesses united!

Afflictions and evils exist not for thy members, for they are not of thy creation.

Oh thou, our chief, turn again thy face toward us,--thou mighty one, great one among the gods!

The path that is visible to thee is one that cannot be described, oh thou child Hunnu,

For it doth remain, though thou goest forth through heaven and earth with thy attributes!

Lo, thou art as the Bull of the two goddesses--come thou, child growing in peace, our lord!

Behold us! Thy essence existeth with us like as the essence of Tebba existeth in the place of his destruction.

Come thou in peace, oh great child of his father Mentu!

Within thy temple fear thou not:

Thy son Horus avengeth thee, and he woundeth and carrieth away him who lurked in his den,

He whose name a daily flame destroyeth from among the gods--Tebha 20 perisheth as waste matter.

As for thee, thou hast thy temple

Therein fear thou not Set, nor every calamity done by him or brought about by him.

Nut 21 proceedeth forth, and embraceth thee with joyfulness;

Travel thou through the land among us, odorous at thy coming forth.

Rebels behold us gazing upon thy face, glowing in its marvellousness.

Behold! our lord is upon our left hand, and behold the beautiful face of the beloved lord turned toward us!

Lo! the Bull, begotten of the two cows Isis and Nephthys!

Lo! there cometh the bearer of the bronze-coloured sistrum, as the praises increase;

Beautiful when he beholdeth him, the lord, among the seated ones,--

He, the progeny of the two cows Isis and Nephthys, the child surpassingly beautiful!

He appeareth unto us in thy image, like the one beloved.

Behold thou me, thy sister Isis, loved of thy heart, loved by thy body;

Loved art thou, because of the inundation of the land this day.

Travel thou among us, oh thou praised one,--

Raise us living in place of what thou hast made empty.

Come thou in peace, oh our lord, whom we behold; our prince!

Approach in peace; drive away tempest from before our temple;

Send thy protection over us like a male protector (Repeat.)

Lo! the two goddesses! Behold Osiris, bull of Amentit, who is alone established!

Very great is he among the gods; the virile infant, the great heir of Sab, 22 born the image of the God of Gods!

Come thou to the two widowed goddesses

There goeth about thee the whole, circle of the gods, and they meet with thee!

Behold, Set 23 cometh--grievous is his name when uttered near thy shrine, in presence of thy father, oh Ra;--

He is cast forth to contend with opponents

Come surely to thy priests, striving and grieving before thy temple;

Come surely to thy priests, in none other than thine own image!

Our lord sitteth down in his temple in peace alone; the great conqueror is his name.

After his long suffering he resteth, taking dangerous council against his enemies

He smiteth the land in his designs.

Go forth, great one with the gods;

And with thee the circle of the gods in front, with the instrument-for-opening-the-mouth, 24 that it may equal thy perfection before the gods.

Walk through the land entirely, great one which art a body, with the royal Uraeus upon his forehead.

He is carried within his heart;

At his coming, the whole speech of the god loved alone is found; his soul is exceedingly beloved.

Live thou in repeated union with the two goddesses;

Thy arms shall attain their desire now as formerly;

Thou hast proclaimed thyself under thy signet as a king of the circle of the gods--the lord!

Thy priests surely come; thy father Ra smiteth that which hath evil designs.

The circle of the gods surroundeth thy pathway, and they meet with thee:

Destroy thou the evil ones and the great calamity which has fallen upon the two counterparts, Isis and Nephthys:

Thy house is holding festival for the calamity (of evil-doers).

His enemies are cut off by disaster from him, when they behold him:

He overfloweth the land as is his custom.

He hath driven away disaster from Nut; the surface, of the earth hath he laid bare, and carried it away in his chariot:

He hath carried away and smitten the enemies of thy father, oh Ra, to justify himself. Thy son Horus is fettered so that he may not answer to thee:

Traverse thou the land in thy manifestations, stride thou like Nut over the four quarters of the world.

Thou passest over the land, above the godly temples of the two goddesses, Isis and Nephthys:

At thy proceeding thou art exalted twice over.

Behold, Set in his chariot--thy enemies are not his enemies!

Come thou into thy temple, oh Osiris, and seek for thy place;

Behold thou, and hearken to the speech of Horus, lying in the arms of his mother, Isis:

Overcome thou indeed in the two lands, oh lord!

Carry out thy word, preserve it in the temple, inscribe thou it, oh great God;

Restrain with thy manifestations, in thy going forth from thy temple, oh Osiris!

Come thou in peace to thy seat, oh lord, Conqueror!

Show us the great Bull, the lovable lord, as he shall become!

Thy duck, thy sister, Isis, produceth the sweet odours belonging to thee and with thee,

Yet thy way doth not tend toward us, oh our lord!

Give thou life from the beginning unto believers!

Hail! Guard thou the inundation in the land of Tesdu, 25 like as thou hast never done before!

Thy sister cometh to thee; she openeth for thee her arms, oh great god, living, great, beloved!

She dandleth thy son in front of thee, at the head of the south and the north!

The lord of ornamentation, the great male one in the heaven of the gods, is decorated!

Thou camest from thy mother, Nut; she spread herself out before thee at thy coming forth from her;

She protected thy limbs from all evil; she followed thee as her babe.

She drove away every danger from thy limbs, chiefly that which was harmful to thee, thou child, the lord.

He goeth forth from Nut; he gazeth upon this land as its head, he the only lord, the child!

Thou goest forth from this cow which conceiveth from the gods, oh thou opener of the underworld in its time!

Lo! the child followeth; thy father Ra remains not;

Thy son Horus shall take vengeance for thee upon the enemy for every calamity brought about by him.

Come thou to thy temple, and fear thou not!

Come thou to thy temple, and fear thou not!

Behold the two impersonators of the goddesses behold the excellent sistrum-bearers!

Approach to thy temple! Be thou exalted twice over in thy temple!

Lo, the gods are in their places! I am the glorious sister of her elder brother!

Thy wife, the elder of thy mother!

Come thou to me, running after my heart, which would look upon thee;

Thy back hath never been beheld by me-make clear the way to us, before me.

Behold Ra in heaven! Protect, oh Nut, the land!

Make a shadow in the land as doth Ra: inflame the heart, that thou mayest escape evil:

Inflame the heart, to cause thee to come after me!

Lo! thou canst not prevent it from turning me toward thee.

Firm are the dwellings of Osiris returning on his paths!

I am seeking after love: behold me existing in the city, great are its walls,

I grieve for thy love toward me-come thou only, now that thou hast departed!

Behold thy son, who causeth Tebha 26 to retreat from destruction!

Hidden am I among the plants, and concealed is thy son that he cannot answer to thee, while this great calamity remaineth!

Yet concerning thee, there is no likeness of thy flesh left:

I follow thee alone and surround the plants, each of which holdeth danger for thy son,--

Lo, I, a woman, in front of all!

Behold this male child! Lo, I know, I and the Opener-of-Ways, Osiris.

I go about thy ways, I turn back towards my elder brother, escaping from danger.

I inflame the hearts of hundreds of thousands, and ponder greatly upon the gods.

Behold us, oh lord! let thy love not lack before our faces, thou male one, sweet lord, ruler of Egypt, lord eternal!

Fly thou with life, prince everlasting; destroy the ones who know not the goddess, thou ruler of Upper and Lower Egypt, the lord!

Command over Deseret: 27 --there thou remainest not,

For full of me is the heart which existeth in him, the elder, the lord!

Command over the Nome of Iqertet! 28

Come to me with thy attributes Come in peace!

Come in peace, oh ruler of Upper and Lower Egypt, thou prince!

Come in peace because of our love for thee--come like the breath, like my love at beholding thee!

My arms are raised for thy protection; love thou me!

Love thou me in the two orbits of the Realms of Osiris, full of my pondering about thee!

There thou dost receive a fillet for the hair among them who dwell therein;

Breezes blow for thee with perfume, oh husband, elder, lord beloved!

Come thou in peace to thy temple--lo, the excellent sistrum-bearer approacheth to thy house, with his instrument of music on his arm. (Repeat twice.)

Thou dost take from thy shrine thy possessions as the male one of Amentit, the place of thy shrine;

Thy body is before the temple of Hennu. Hail! in thy name of prince everlasting!

Horus cometh to thee in strength;

He removeth thy limbs and he collecteth thine emanations and that which goeth forth from thee:

The great god approacheth at thy word, and is restrained by thy attributes.

Come thou in peace, oh our lord, the child, for continually thy son Horus doth avenge thee.

Come before thy temple-grant abundance to thy holy temple which thou lovest, oh prince, leader, strong one!

Break open before us as the only Egg, oh strong one, valorous son!

Lo, this one is the opener-of-the-body, the masterful one--the god Seb is before his mother.

Great are my adornings, for that done in Amentit is beloved:

He hath vanquished disaster, he is lord of the dead, the Bull of Amentit, born of Horus-Ra of the two horizons, the child lovely to the one beholding him.

Come thou to us in peace twice renewed--remove thou thy penalties;

Drive away the evil moment, oh our lord!

Come thou to us in peace twice renewed! Praise the child!

The elder cometh in peace, rejoicing, and there cometh the looked-for ruler of Egypt, the prince eternal, as "Still Heart." 29

As "Still Heart" is thy heart, oh our lord; come thou to thy temple--fear thou not the great evils.

Dost thou not behold and hear the words uttered at thy Heb-festival?

Behold, the excellent sistrum-bearer!

There cometh to thy temple the circle of the gods, seeking to see thee, oh child, lord, first maker of the body.

The babe whom thou lovest is before thy face, the heir overcoming at the beginning, the excellent son.

There proccedeth from the temple, visibly and audibly, the grieving of Isis concerning thee, upon the path to thy place.

Grant deliverance before those whom thou lovest

They weep for thee with hair unbound,--before Un-Nofer, the lord of bounty, the prince great in his terror, the god above the heavens!

The gods produce the inundation for thee--begotten is it by thee daily.

Lo! the divine essence of the gods is spread upon his limbs:

Behold! he causeth to live those of the older time and human beings since,--he the lord of bounty, prince making fertile,

Great lord, plant giving life, granting twice over the peace of the gods!

There are funeral offerings for the souls of the deceased, and for Seshta, 30 the lord of the funeral couch, the lord of the sacred eye, in the holy horizon of the temple.

He shineth at his season, and is brilliant in his hour,--

Thou art Khu, who art accompanied by radiances.

Shine thou at the left hand of Tum--

Behold, thou art upon the seat of Ra, revealing his brilliances.

Thy mummy flieth with thy soul toward Ra.

Thou illuminest at the daybreak, and thou restest at evening, this being thy daily work;

For thou art at the left hand of Tum the everlasting, eternal. Thou risest, and hateful wickedness is restrained even before it is conceived) before its calamity cometh upon thee.

He turneth back the attack of foes that come fiercely against him.

The god Imsehti, 31 he is thy heir;

Cause thou every one of the gods to praise him.

Exalt the circle of the gods by thy victory occupy thyself with Ra every day.

Behold thou the image on thy left hand--behold thou the image of living beings, for thou art Tum, the forerunner of Ra.

There cometh to thee the entire circle of the gods above thy head, invoking joy upon thy head, and falling flame upon thine enemies.

There is praise to thee from us, that thy flesh may embrace again thy bones; thy word is decreed every day.

Approach. thou like Tum in his season, turning not: thy sinews are strong in thee, oh thou Opener-of-Ways!

He bringeth thee to the mountains, he heweth the place of burial;

There belongeth to thee all Ta-Deseret. 32

For thee are the two, Isis and Nephthys--do thou strengthen us, for they ponder on thy image.

Thy limbs are as mutilated unto thee; they seek to bind together thy dead body.

No calamity cometh to them when approaching to thee with hair unbound!

Come thou to us entirely, for thou rememberest

Thou comest with thy attributes before the land modify thy power.

For thy peace is proclaimed to us, oh lord, heir of the two thrones, god alone excellent, designed of the gods: every god adoreth thee!

Thou comest; it is thy temple; fear not, beloved of Ra, beloved of thy two images;

Be peaceful in thy temple; thy words are eternal!

Lo! the two representatives of the goddesses! Lo! the excellent sistrum-bearer!

Come to thy temple--he rejoiceth twice over in thy temple because of thee, oh child, like one beloved!

Behold thou! Come, come to us: great is thy protection, thou whom we love: come thou to thy temple, nor fear thou.

Behold the gods existing in heaven! Behold the gods existing on earth!

Behold the gods existing in the Place of the Dead! Behold the gods existing in the expanse of the universe!

Come after us who are under thy lady, every one beloved by thee, the eldest-born, lord of love; to him be praise!

Come to me, thou uniter of heaven to earth, who causeth his shadow daily in the land, messenger of heaven to earth!

Hail! Approach thou to us with me, eldest-born wife, in the city!

Seek for our lord-traverse the land toward our lord!

Come to me, thou messenger of heaven, who changeth things:

Cause the god to come to his house, breathing again with the breath of thy nostrils!

Behold! the breath from the lord is in his great temple!

Praise Ra, the avenger; he doth not oppose that which is thine; but he hath produced calamity after the desire of thy heart!

Behold thou, rejoicing king, beautiful child! Hail oh lord beloved!

Come to me, oh lord; thou who art beheld daily, thou elder one!

Come, behold us; great are thy two arms! Lo! thine avenger! The two arms lift thee up twice over!

They are thy protection, male, lord, child, babe!

It is the avenger, our lord--lo, I am son of Seb!

Depart not from me in thy time-lo! it is not ever his time!

I follow after thy ways, after thy going thence, lord beloved of me;

Thou who hoverest over the lands, nor restest in thy passage:

I am inflamed with loving thee! Hail! Approach!

Behold, I weep for thee alone; come to me who runneth because of my desire to behold thee;

While I am behind thee I desire to behold thy face!

Hail, thou who art invoked in thy temple, being protected twice over in peace!

Hail to thee twice over! Our lord cometh to his temple; our arms shall protect him behind his temple.

Our lord cometh in peace to his place: when thou art established in thy temple, fear thou not!

Lo! praised twice over is our lord, with acclamation, because God is great.

Come thou in peace and truth; go thou forth under Ra, masterful among the gods, approved one!

Come in Peace, thou looked-for child!

Come thou with thy attributes as a child the evil one has fallen; Horus is as a prince.

He is great toward thee; he is not exalted above thee in his circuit.

Lo, the two goddesses, the ones loving the father, lord of rejoicings!

The hearts of the circle of the gods of the region of Fayûm rejoice for thee;

Thy holy temple holdeth thy beauties; the circle of the gods is filled with awe at thy terribleness and the land trembleth at thy terror.

I am thy wife, made as thou art, the elder sister, soul of her brother.

He cometh and is visible, the lord beloved, praised twice over, the great Egg.

He cometh and is visible, the babe; the child advanceth, he cometh and is visible.

The extent of the earth weepeth for thee; the regions lament for thee, Seshta; 33

Heaven and earth weep for thee, for great art thou among the gods

There are not a few who adore thy soul--come to thy temple, nor fear thou.

Thy son Horus embraceth the circuit of heaven; Bebi 34 prevaileth; fear thou not.

Thy son Horus taketh vengeance before thee; he overthroweth for thee the evil ones and plotters.

Hail, oh lord, whose increase in brightness is daily beheld; the odour of thy limbs is like odours of Punt.

Praised are those who are dead and at peace and the entire circle of the gods rejoiceth.

Come thou to thy wife in peace; her heart fluttereth for thy love; she is not embraced since thy going from her.

Her heart shall delight to behold thee--thy beauties go forth of thee to her in thy shrine.

She removeth from thy limbs calamity and evil, such as hath never happened unto thee formerly.

Come thou to life in front of thy wife! Hail!

Guard thou the inundation in the fields of Aphroditopolis this day--grant grain twice over--let there be no likeness of evil.

The Cow 35 weepeth for thee with her voice; thou art beloved in her heart; her heart fluttereth, enchanted for thee;

She embraceth thy limbs with her two arms, and cometh running steadily toward thee, for peace.

Behold, her vengeance is accomplished for thee she is caused to be mighty by thee;

Thy flesh hath she bound with thy bones for thee; she hath gathered for thee thy breath in front of thee, and made thy bones entire.

Thy mother Nut cometh to thee in peace, she hath built up life from her own body

The renewed soul is made doubly steadfast--thy soul it is, oh male begotten, lord of women!

There is unguent for the hair at thy coming to the regions of the gods--

Unguent for thine anointed hair. Lo, he goeth forth himself--he cometh

Come in peace twice over, King of Egypt, prince!

Come in peace, lord of Sais; her 36 two arms are stretched toward thee, oh Shenthit, 37 and her heart goeth forth to thee!

Thou art as God--come forth with godly amulets, for lo! they are not over his child to protect him.

Thy hair is like turquoise over his body, at thy coming into the cultivated fields:

With turquoise is thy hair twined and with lapis lazuli, the finest of lapis lazuli:

Lo! the lapis lazuli is above thy hair: thy skin and thy flesh are like iron of the south thy bones are formed of silver.

I am as a child: thy teeth are to thee as fine lapis lazuli:

Sweet-scented odours are upon thy hair, with unguents that proceed from himself.

Chiefs are before thee as lapis lazuli. Sab lifts up himself with offerings unto thee, causing him, the great God, to approach,

He, who goeth forth in front of the great heir, who goeth forth from Ra, the eldest one, beautiful prince, of god-like face, the living soul of Istennu (Thoth)--

The child, proceeding from the God of seeing and hearing, the eldest one, prince of eastern

and western horizons, heir of Sab.

He giveth to thee every circuit of the Sun God Aten--come to thy temple, oh Osiris, Opener-of-Ways to the Gods:

Thou openest thy two eyes and thou dost behold among them.

Remove thou storms of rain and give thou sunshine to the land, with fecundity during the night-time.

Come to thy temple, oh Osiris Khent-Amentit; come to thy temple!

Come with the body of the Uraeus on thy head: his two eyes shine over the two regions of the gods;

Exalted twice over is the prince, our lord.

Thy foes are destined for slaughter, since they are not steadfast at all because of thy name.

Make firm thy limbs for thee, oh Un-Nofer--life, stability and health;

For thy flesh causeth the heart to rest, oh Osiris, beautiful.

Lo, there goeth forth with thee, and in front of thee, this god Hu, 38 and Tatenen, thy father, who supporteth heaven; and thou art the fourth god who progresseth therein.

Thy soul flyeth to the east, because thou art as the image of Ra.

Those existing in the realms of the dead are accepted with rejoicing:

Sab, who existeth therein, openeth unto thee.

They come to thee with an offering, and travel to thee with an offering from Deddu. 39

Osiris is exalted before thee--he is exalted twice over in peace.

There cometh unto thee Isis, lady of the horizon, who hath begotten herself alone in the image of the gods.

It is she who is avenged before thee--it is she who is avenged before thee!

She hath taken vengeance before Horus, the woman who was made a male by her father Osiris.

Go forth and behold the "Opener-of-Ways," 40 the revered, the Uraeus-wearer!

Come forth as Ra; come forth as the pupil of the eye that beholdeth Tum, when Ra shineth as chief twice over!

Behold! He cometh!

COLOPHON

This litany compiled by the priest of the temple of Het, 41 the Recorder of Amen of the rank of Sa, 42 the priest Nes-Amsu, son of the priest Pedi-Amen, for the King of the two lands, he being the sistrum-bearer of Amen-Ra, and son of Ta-Mut, she who belongeth to Tunra.

Writings of the 12th year, 4th month of summer, in the day of the Pharaoh (life, stability and health) Alexander, 43 son of Alexander, prince of the god and father;--he being also priest of Amen-Ra, king of the Gods, priest of Horus the Ra, the great child, supreme, firstborn of Amen; priest of the Amen-of-the-two-Horus, priest of Khensu in the midst of Bennit, 44 priest of Osiris-of-the-great-persea-trees, priest of Osiris-in-the-midst-of-Ishrel, priest of Amen-haset-in-the-midst-of-Ipui, Uab-priest of the Ra in the chief temple of the temples of Amen, over the Sa-priests of second rank; recorder of the treasury of the God Amen, over the Sa-priests of second rank; deputy of Amen, of the Sa-priests of second and fourth rank; priest of Nofer-Hotep, the great God; priest of Nofer-Hotep the child, priest of Osiris, Horus, Isis and Nephthys, priest of the temple of Het, priest of Amsu; priest of Hathor, lady of Het-Sekhem; 45 priest of Mehyt, priest of Tum, lord of Het-Sekhem, deputy of Nofer-Hotep of the four grades of Sa-priests, priest of the chief of Nofer-Hotep, priest of the Gods.

16 Title of Osiris--"Within the underworld."

17 Officiates at Heb-festival.

18 Sun god.

19 Osiris.

20 Name of Set.

21 Goddess of night, mother of Osiris.

22 God of earth, father of Osiris.

23 Sutekh.

24 Religious ceremony.

25 Aphroditopolis

26 Set.

27 Land of the dead.

28 Underworld.

29 Osiris.

30 One of the gods of the underworld.

31 God of light.

32 Land of the Dead.

33 Here used for Osiris.

34 Son of Osiris.

35 Hathor.

36 *I.e.* the City›s.

37 Osiris.

38 A god of earth.

39 The Celestial City.

40 Osiris.

41 Diospolis Parva.

42 Priest's grade.

43 Alexander II, son of Philip Aridaeus.

44 Part of Thebes.

45 Capital of VII Nome, Upper Egypt.

Hymn To Osiris-Sokar

FORMULAE for the bringing in of Osiris-Sokar, in connection with the mysteries spoken heretofore.

Hail, royal one, coming forth in the body!

Hail, hereditary son, chief of the ranks of the gods!

Hail, lord of many existences!

Hail, thou whose substance is like gold in the temples!

Hail, lord of the duration of life, giver of years!

Hail, lord living throughout eternity!

Hail, lord worthy of many hundreds of thousands of praises!

Hail, brilliant one, both at thy rising and thy setting!

Hail to him who maketh pleasant all that which breatheth!

Behold the lord of great fear and trembling

Hail, lord of many divinities!

Hail, resplendent one-with the white crown, lord of the royal crown!

Behold the sacred child of Horus, the praised one!

Hail, thou soul of Ra, in the adored boat

Hail, thou restful leader! take possession of thy shrine.

Behold the lord of fear, who causeth himself to come into being!

Hail, thou whose heart palpitateth not,--take possession of thy city!

Behold the one beloved of gods and goddesses

Hail, thou who causeth the inundation,--take possession of thy temple!

Hail, dweller in the underworld,--take possession of thy offerings!

Hail, thou protector,--take possession of thy temple!

Hail, thou who growest like unto the ape of Tehuti, or to the shining sunlight!

Hail, thou flower honoured of Pharaoh!

Hail, thou who handlest the holy rigging of the Sektet-boat!46

Behold the lord of youth,--he becometh old in his shrine!

Behold the excellent souls, which are in the realms of Death!

Behold the sacred designer of north and south!

Behold the mysterious one, lie who is unknown to mankind!

Rail, thou enlightener of those who are in the underworld, that they may see the sunlight!

Behold the lord of the Atef crown, the great one in Suten-Henen!

Hail, thou great and terrible one of Naret!

Hail, dweller in Uast,47 flourishing for ever!

Hail, Amen-Ra, King of the Gods, who causeth his members to grow in his rising and in his setting!

Hail, receiver of monuments and offerings at the entrance of the tomb!

Hail, thou who placest the Uraeus crown upon the head of its lord!

Hail, thou who causest the earth to remain in its place!

Rail, opener of the mouth of the four great gods who are in the underworld!

Rail, living soul of Osiris, crowning him with the moon!

Hail, thou who dost hide his essence in the great shrine of Amen!

Hail, thou hidden God, Osiris in the underworld!

Hail, thou whose soul resteth in heaven,--whose enemy hath fallen!

The Goddess Isis speaketh unto thee, uttering a cry from the river--

"Send the purified 'Abd'-fish from before the boat of Ra, oh lord of the beginning,

Who becometh like the immortal ones that rejoice,--thou egg who becometh as one renewed."

She cutteth off the heads of the enemies in this her name of "Lady of Tepka."

Oh, lady of the beginning, come thou before our faces in this her name of Hathor, lady of emerald, lady of Uast the holy!

Come thou in peace, because of this her name of Hathor, lady of Uast the holy!

Come thou in peace, oh Tayt, in this her name of lady of peace!

Come thou in front, to overthrow her enemy, in this her name of Hathor, lady of the temple of Suten-Henen, the golden!

Come thou in peace, in this her name of Hathor, lady of Inbut!

Come thou in peace beside Neb-er-zer in this name of Hathor, lady of Shet-Tekh!

Shine, oh golden one, beside her father in this her name of Bast.

Go forward over the temples and by the side of the great temple, in this her name of Satet.

The two lands become fertile,--regulate thou the gods in this her name of Mazit.

Hathor overpowereth the enemy of her father by this her name of Sekhet!

Mazit overpowereth exceedingly in this her name of lady of Immu.

She placeth perfume upon her head and her hair, in this her name of Neit.

Extol him before the gods, and before his witnesses!

Hathor is the lady of Uast Hathor is the lady of Suten-Henen:

Hathor is the lady of Tepka Hathor is the lady of Mehut:

Hathor is the lady of Rehesau: Hathor is the lady of Shet-Desret:

Hathor is the lady of the Turquoise: Hathor is the lady of Ineb:

Hathor is the lady of Uahwah: Hathor is the lady of Ammu:

Hathor is the lady of Imem: Hathor is as Hennu of Met-Sas!

The nine companions48 approach--let your arms be beneath your father Osiris--protect the land. (Repeat four times.)

Hail, thou crowned lord of the feast! (Repeat twice.)

Oh prince! hail! it is sweet for the courtesans whom thou lovest!

Hail, thou who livest twice over throughout eternity!

Hail!-thou keepest festival for ever!

Hail, adored one: thou advancest along the ways!

Hail, thou who art established in the regions above the heavens!

Hail, oh God,--hear thou! Protect the land!

Hear thou the cry--protect the land from the gates of the heavenly nomes!

Hail to him who cometh forth with his two eyes, son of the servant of God!,

Hail, protector, preserver when thou speakest!

Hail, protector of Pharaoh, when be doeth what thou lovest!

Hail, protector of Pharaoh, when he causeth thy praises to be made!

Hail, thou seated one, for there cometh to thee this peace of heart!

Hail to the son of--the servant of God--there is recited for him the service of the festival!

Hail, thou who art established by the name of Deddu-above-the-heavens!

Hail, thou sweet-scented one in Deddu-above-the-heavens!

Hail, thou who comest subduing hostile ones

Hail, thou who comest adoring the Infant!

Hail, thou who producest his fear in rebellious hearts!

Hail, oh worker who followeth his lord, though the follower of the god Bast attendeth him not!

Behold, there are rebellious hearts, hating the temple, but the end of all things strikes them upon their necks!

Lo! the coming of the lord of Deddu-above-the heavens--he strikes down rebellious hearts! (Repeat the words sixteen times to the accompaniment of musical instruments.)

It is finished.

COLOPHON

May their names remain fixed, and not destroyed for ever before Osiris, Horus, Isis, Nephthys--those gods and goddesses who are herein mentioned;. and before the gods and goddesses in their entirety who are in the underworld, and in the chambers and great shrines existing in the underworld.

Lo! may they cause to come forth these names existent in the underworld in excellence! Let them be invoked in the Nai-boat49 of Ra. Let there be given for them funereal offerings upon the altar of the great God, day by day!

Let there be given for them cool water, and incense as to the excellent kings of Upper and Lower Egypt, who are existent in the underworld. Let them be permitted to go out and come in among those praised of Osiris, who is the breath of those in the underworld. Let it be caused that the beams of Aten50 may fall upon their bodies every day.

If there be any man--any one of this land, or any one, Negro, Kushite or Syrian, who removeth this writing, or carrieth it away as a thief, let none approach to them, nor give to them of cooling water; nor let them breathe the zephyrs; nor permit to remain to them son nor daughter of their begetting, nor let the name of such a one be mentioned in the land if they be born, nor let them behold the beams of the sun.

But if there be a man, any one whomsoever, who beholdeth this writing and causeth my soul and my name to become established among those who are blessed, let it be done for him likewise after his final arriving (at the end of life's voyage) in recompense for what was done by him for me, Osiris.

46 Boat of the Dead.

47 Thebes.

48 The Paut, or circle of the gods.

49 To carry souls.

50 Sun God.